7 Businesses to **Avoid** and
4 **Winning** Opportunities

BUSINESS SUCCESS GUIDE

By Elisabeth Miazello

Copyright © 2024 Elisabeth Miazello. All rights reserved.

No part of this publication may be reproduced, distributed, or transmitted in any form or by any means, including photocopying, recording, or other electronic or mechanical methods, without the prior written permission of the publisher, except in the case of brief quotations embodied in critical reviews and certain other noncommercial uses permitted by copyright law. For permission requests, write to the publisher, addressed "Attention: Permissions Coordinator," at the address below.

Disclaimer:
The information provided in this book is for general informational purposes only. All information in the book is provided in good faith, however, we make no representation or warranty of any kind, express or implied, regarding the accuracy, adequacy, validity, reliability, availability, or completeness of any information in the book.

Under no circumstance shall we have any liability to you for any loss or damage of any kind incurred as a result of the use of the book or reliance on any information provided in the book. Your use of the book and your reliance on any information in the book is solely at your own risk.

This book is not intended to serve as professional or legal advice. You should seek the advice of professionals, as appropriate, regarding the evaluation of any specific information, opinion, advice, or other content.

Dear Reader,

Thank you so much for taking the time to read "7 **Businesses to Avoid and 4 Winning Opportunities: Your Business Success Guide.**" I hope you found the insights and strategies helpful in your journey to making informed business decisions.

Your support means the world to me, and I truly appreciate your interest in my work. It's readers like you who inspire me to continue sharing knowledge and helping others navigate the complex world of business.

If you enjoyed this book and found it valuable, I would be incredibly grateful if you could take a moment to leave a review. Your feedback helps other readers discover this book and benefits the entire community of aspiring entrepreneurs.

Author Page

To leave a review on Amazon, just scan the code above or visit

Elisabeth Miazello Amazon Profile:
https://www.amazon.com/author/elisabeth.miazello

Leaving a review is simple and only takes a few minutes. Your honest thoughts and experiences will be immensely helpful. Thank you once again for your support. Wishing you all the best on your business journey!

Warm regards,
Elisabeth Miazello

Ready to Transform Your Future?

Grab your **FREE eBook** now and discover:

7 Businesses You Can Start Right Now for Under $1000

Don't miss out on this opportunity to kickstart your entrepreneurial journey!

Scan the **QR Code** Above or Visit **IRNOX.com/7a** for an <u>Instant Free Download</u>

Take the first step towards financial freedom.

Table of Contents:

Introduction 6

Chapter 1: Gyms 8

Chapter 2: ATMs 12

Chapter 3: Dry Cleaners 16

Chapter 4: Hotels 20

Chapter 5: Amazon FBA 24

Chapter 6: Retail Stores 28

Chapter 7: Restaurants 32

Chapter 8: Trucking and Last Mile Delivery 37

Chapter 10: Real Estate Rental Properties 43

Chapter 11: Laundromats 49

A Guide to Choosing the Best Business 55

Introduction

Welcome, future entrepreneurs and savvy business minds! If you've ever dreamed of starting your own business but felt paralyzed by the fear of failure, you're not alone. In fact, did you know that 66% of would-be entrepreneurs never take the plunge because they're too scared of failing? That's a staggering number! But here's the good news: you've just taken a crucial step towards overcoming that fear by picking up this eBook.

Why This eBook?

So, what's in it for you? Why should you invest your precious time in reading this guide? Well, here's the deal: this eBook is designed to be your roadmap to success. We've done the heavy lifting by diving deep into the data, analyzing which businesses have the highest and lowest failure rates. The goal? To arm you with the knowledge you need to make an informed decision about where to invest your time, money, and energy.

What Value Will You Gain?

- **Clarity and Confidence:** No more guesswork. You'll understand exactly which types of businesses are more likely to thrive and which ones to approach with caution.
- **Strategic Insights:** We break down the reasons why some businesses fail and others succeed. By

learning from these insights, you can avoid common pitfalls and set yourself up for success.
- **Actionable Advice:** Each chapter is packed with practical tips and strategies that you can apply to your own business journey. Whether you're eyeing a high-risk venture or a more stable opportunity, you'll find valuable guidance here.
- **Real Examples:** We provide real-world examples to illustrate key points, making the content relatable and easy to digest.

Let's Get Started

In the pages that follow, we'll explore a variety of businesses, from gyms and ATMs to senior care centers and rental properties. You'll learn why some of these ventures have alarmingly high failure rates, while others are surprisingly resilient. By the end of this eBook, you'll have a clear understanding of which business model aligns best with your goals and risk tolerance.

Chapter 1: Gyms

The Allure and the Reality

Starting a gym might sound like a dream come true for fitness enthusiasts. Imagine transforming your passion for fitness into a thriving business, helping others achieve their health goals while staying fit yourself. It sounds perfect, right? Unfortunately, the reality is quite different. In fact, gyms have one of the highest failure rates among new businesses, with a staggering 80% not making it past their first year.

Why Gyms Fail ?

Let's break down why so many gyms don't succeed:

1. Financial Mismanagement:

Many gym owners dive into the business with enthusiasm but without a solid financial plan. Managing cash flow, understanding expenses, and setting realistic revenue goals are crucial. Without these, it's easy to run out of money quickly.

2. Poor Marketing:

You can have the best gym in town, but if no one knows about it, it won't matter. Many gym owners don't invest enough in marketing or don't know how to effectively attract and retain members.

3. Inconsistent Pricing:

Custom pricing and a lack of standardization can confuse potential customers. A clear, attractive pricing structure is essential for drawing in and keeping clients.

4. Limited Revenue Streams:

Relying solely on memberships can limit your profitability. Successful gyms often sell third-party products, offer high-margin services like personal training, and run classes or events that engage members and generate extra income.

Successful Gym Models

Despite the high failure rate, not all gym businesses are doomed. There are models that have proven to be successful:

1. Low-Cost Subscription Gyms:

Gyms like Planet Fitness thrive on a model where they offer memberships at a low price point (around $10 a month). They bank on the idea that many members won't show up regularly, keeping operating costs lower while maintaining a large membership base.

2. High-Cost, High-Engagement Gyms:

Gyms like Equinox charge a premium (around $200-300 a month) but offer a high level of engagement and exclusive services. These gyms focus on creating a luxurious, personalized experience that justifies the higher price tag.

Key Takeaways for Aspiring Gym Owners

If you're still determined to open a gym, here are some tips to help increase your chances of success:

- **Develop a Robust Financial Plan:** Understand your costs, set realistic revenue goals, and keep a close eye on cash flow.
- **Invest in Marketing:** Use social media, local advertising, and promotions to attract and retain members. A strong online presence is crucial.

- **Standardized Pricing:** Make your pricing clear and competitive. Consider offering various membership tiers to appeal to different customers.
- **Diversify Your Revenue Streams:** Don't rely solely on memberships. Sell products, offer personal training, and host events or classes to boost your income.

Starting a gym is not for the faint-hearted. It requires passion, dedication, and a solid business strategy. By understanding the common pitfalls and learning from successful models, you can improve your chances of turning your dream into a profitable reality. Remember, the key to success is not just in the love of fitness but in smart business practices. So, are you ready to pump up your entrepreneurial muscles and take on the challenge?

Chapter 2: ATMs

The Temptation of Easy Money

The idea of owning a fleet of ATMs sounds like a simple, passive income dream. You install a few machines, collect transaction fees, and watch the money roll in while you kick back and relax. But, as with many things that sound too good to be true, the reality of running an ATM business is quite different.

Why ATMs Fail?

Here's a breakdown of why so many ATM ventures don't pan out:

1. Low Transaction Volume:

On average, an ATM processes only three to five transactions a day, each worth about $80 to $100. With typical commissions of 1-2%, you're looking at a meager $2.40 to $15 a day per machine. That's hardly enough to cover your costs, let alone turn a profit.

2. Logistical Challenges:

ATMs need to be regularly stocked with cash, and there's always a risk of theft. This means frequent trips to replenish the machines and ensure their security, which can be time-consuming and costly.

3. High Initial Costs:

ATMs themselves are expensive, and it typically takes about seven years to recoup your initial investment through revenue and profits. That's a long time to wait for a return on your investment.

4. Declining Cash Use:

With the rise of digital payments and a cashless society, fewer people are using cash. This trend poses a significant risk to the ATM business model, as the user base continues to shrink.

5. Low Margins:

The profit margins on ATM transactions are slim. Given the low transaction volumes and high operational costs, it's challenging to sustain the business on a small scale.

Potential Success Models

Despite these challenges, there are scenarios where an ATM business can work:

1. High Cash Usage Locations:

Places like cannabis stores, which often operate on a cash-only basis, or busy bars can ensure high transaction volumes. However, these locations often demand higher rent, which can offset the benefits.

2. Scale Matters:

To make significant profits, you would need to operate a large number of ATMs – think 50 to 100 machines. This requires substantial capital and logistics management, but it can increase your earnings significantly.

Key Takeaways for Aspiring ATM Owners

If you're still interested in venturing into the ATM business, here are some tips to help increase your chances of success:

- **Choose High Traffic Locations:** Focus on placing your ATMs in locations with high foot traffic and cash usage.
- **Consider Partnerships:** Partner with businesses that can benefit from having an ATM on-site, such as convenience stores, bars, or event venues.
- **Plan for Security:** Invest in robust security measures to protect your machines and the cash inside them.
- **Scale Your Business:** Aim to operate a large number of machines to increase your overall transaction volume and profits.

The ATM business, while seemingly straightforward, comes with its own set of challenges and risks. Success requires careful planning, strategic placement, and the ability to manage multiple machines efficiently. If you're up for the challenge and can navigate these hurdles, there's potential to turn a profit. But remember, like any business, it's crucial to understand the risks and plan accordingly.

Chapter 3: Dry Cleaners

The Perceived Stability and Hidden Risks

Dry cleaning businesses might seem like a stable and profitable venture at first glance. After all, people always need clean clothes, right? However, diving into the world of dry cleaners reveals a slew of hidden risks and challenges that make this business much less appealing than it might initially appear.

Why Dry Cleaners Fail?

Let's uncover why so many dry-cleaning businesses end up closing their doors:

1. Declining Demand:

The demand for dry cleaning services has significantly decreased over the years. Here's why:

- Casual Work Attire: With the rise of remote work and more casual dress codes, fewer people are wearing suits and other clothing that require dry cleaning.

- Changing Fashion Trends: Everyday clothing is increasingly made from materials that can be washed at home, reducing the need for dry cleaning services.

2. High Remediation Costs:

One of the biggest financial pitfalls of owning a dry cleaner is the potential for environmental remediation costs. Traditional dry cleaning methods often leave toxic residues in the soil, which the business owner is responsible for cleaning up. Here's why this is problematic:

- Expensive Cleanup: Remediation can cost anywhere from $5,000 to hundreds of thousands of dollars, depending on the extent of contamination.
- Widespread Contamination: The EPA estimates that 75% of dry cleaners in the US are contaminated, meaning most businesses will face these high costs at some point.

3. Financial Pitfalls:

- High Initial Costs: Buying a dry-cleaning business can seem affordable, with prices ranging from $100,000 to $200,000. However, the potential remediation costs make these deals less attractive.
- Low Profit Margins: Most dry cleaners generate modest profits. When you add potential

remediation costs, what seemed like a profitable venture can quickly become a financial burden.

4. Environmental Concerns:

- Sustainability Issues: As society moves towards greener, more sustainable practices, businesses with high environmental risks and costs are becoming less viable. The traditional dry-cleaning process is often at odds with these values.

Key Takeaways for Aspiring Dry Cleaners

If you're still considering entering the dry-cleaning business, here are some tips to help mitigate the risks:

- **Opt for Eco-Friendly Methods:** Consider adopting environmentally friendly cleaning methods that reduce or eliminate toxic residues. This can help lower potential remediation costs and appeal to environmentally conscious consumers.
- **Thoroughly Assess Locations:** Before purchasing a dry cleaning business, conduct thorough environmental assessments to understand potential remediation costs.

- **Diversify Services:** Offer additional services like laundry, alterations, or shoe repair to diversify your revenue streams and attract more customers.

The dry-cleaning business is fraught with hidden challenges that can quickly turn a seemingly stable venture into a financial nightmare. Declining demand, high remediation costs, and environmental concerns make this industry particularly risky. However, with careful planning and a focus on sustainable practices, there is potential to carve out a niche in this market.

Chapter 4: Hotels

The Dream vs. The Reality

Owning a hotel sounds like a glamorous venture. Imagine welcoming guests from all over the world, offering them a comfortable place to stay, and making a handsome profit while doing so. However, the reality of running a hotel is far from this idyllic picture. Hotels are complex businesses with thin margins and high operational demands, making them one of the trickiest ventures to sustain.

Why Hotels Fail?

Let's dig into the reasons why so many hotels struggle to stay afloat:

1. Thin Margins:

Hotels often generate just enough revenue to cover their operating costs. On average, a hotel makes about $94,000 a year in revenue, but the average expenses are around $96,000. This results in a 2% loss. The industry relies heavily on real estate depreciation to turn a profit by reducing tax liabilities. Without this tax benefit, many hotels wouldn't be profitable at all.

2. 24/7 Operations:

Running a hotel means offering round-the-clock service. This includes dealing with customer complaints, emergencies, and maintenance issues at any hour, which can be incredibly demanding and stressful.

3. Complex Operations:

Hotels require a significant number of staff to handle various tasks like housekeeping, maintenance, landscaping, and guest services. The complexity of managing such a large and diverse team increases operational costs and management challenges.

4. Industry Consolidation:

The hotel industry has seen significant consolidation over the years. Today, a handful of major hotel companies control a large portion of the market. This makes it difficult for independent hotels to compete unless they join a franchise.

5. **Financial Pitfalls:**

- **Franchise Costs:** Approximately 67% of hotels are franchised. Franchise fees can take a substantial portion of your revenue, leaving independent operators with only 2-7% of the total revenue.
- **Long-Term Contracts:** Franchise contracts typically last 10 to 15 years. If the franchise doesn't perform well, you're stuck with it for the duration of the contract.

Key Takeaways for Aspiring Hotel Owners

If you're still keen on entering the hotel business, here are some strategies to help increase your chances of success:

- Choose Your Location Wisely: Location is crucial. High-traffic areas with tourist attractions or business hubs can increase your occupancy rates.
- Consider Boutique Hotels: Smaller, boutique hotels that offer a unique experience can differentiate you from the big chains and attract a niche market.
- Leverage Technology: Use technology to streamline operations, enhance guest experience, and reduce costs. Online booking systems, smart room controls, and customer service apps can make a big difference.

- Focus on Customer Service: Exceptional customer service can lead to positive reviews and repeat business. Invest in training your staff to ensure every guest has a memorable stay.

The hotel business is not for the faint-hearted. It demands a significant investment of time, money, and effort, and the margins are often razor-thin. However, with the right strategies and a focus on providing a unique and exceptional guest experience, it is possible to carve out a successful niche in this industry.

Chapter 5: Amazon FBA

The Allure of the Amazon Empire

The idea of selling products on Amazon through their Fulfillment by Amazon (FBA) program is incredibly enticing. Imagine reaching millions of customers without worrying about storage, shipping, or customer service. It sounds like a dream come true for aspiring entrepreneurs. However, the reality of running an Amazon FBA business is riddled with risks and challenges that make success far from guaranteed.

Why Amazon FBA Fails?

Let's dive into why so many Amazon FBA sellers struggle to find success:

1. Platform Risk:

Amazon itself poses the biggest threat to your business. Here's why:

- Amazon as a Competitor: Amazon can decide to sell a similar product, often at a lower price, leveraging their vast resources and market dominance.

- Chinese Knockoffs: The platform is flooded with cheaper, often inferior knockoff products from overseas manufacturers, making it hard to compete.
- Data Sharing: Amazon can share your sales data with competitors and use it to introduce competing products.

2. Customer Disconnect:

When you sell through Amazon, you lose direct contact with your customers, which has several drawbacks:

- Lack of Customer Data: You don't get access to your customers' contact information, making it impossible to build a direct relationship or gather feedback.
- Restricted Communication: Amazon prohibits sellers from including promotional materials or requests for reviews in the packaging, further distancing you from your customers.

3. Low Success Rate:

The numbers reveal a bleak picture for Amazon FBA sellers:

- High Failure Rate: Only 1% of Amazon sellers achieve annual sales of $100,000 to $250,000.
- Minimal Earnings: 27% of sellers make about $5,000 in total sales, which is barely enough to cover costs, let alone make a profit.

4. Financial Pitfalls:

- Algorithm Dependence: Your product's visibility heavily depends on Amazon's algorithm. A single change can drastically affect your sales and rankings.
- Fake Reviews: Competitors can sabotage your listings with fake reviews, severely damaging your reputation. Negative reviews are particularly harmful, requiring numerous positive reviews to counteract their impact.

Key Takeaways for Aspiring Amazon FBA Sellers

If you're still considering venturing into the Amazon FBA world, here are some tips to help navigate the challenges:

- **Differentiate Your Product:** Offer a unique product that stands out from the competition. High-quality, niche products tend to perform better.
- **Build a Brand:** Focus on creating a strong brand identity. This can help you stand out and build customer loyalty, even on a platform like Amazon.
- **Leverage Multiple Channels:** Don't rely solely on Amazon. Use other sales channels like your own website, social media, and other marketplaces to diversify your revenue streams.

- **Stay Informed:** Keep up with Amazon's policies, algorithms, and market trends. Being adaptable and informed can help you stay ahead of changes.

The Amazon FBA business model, while attractive on the surface, comes with significant risks and a low success rate. It requires careful planning, constant vigilance, and a strong strategy to navigate the platform's challenges. However, with the right approach, it is possible to carve out a profitable niche on Amazon.

Chapter 6: Retail Stores

The Charm and the Challenge

The idea of owning a charming little boutique or a bustling shop on Main Street has a timeless appeal. Retail stores have been a cornerstone of local economies and community life for centuries. However, the modern retail landscape is fraught with challenges that make success elusive for many store owners. Despite the nostalgic charm, the reality of running a retail store is a constant battle against high costs, declining foot traffic, and complex inventory management.

Why Retail Stores Fail?

Let's break down why so many retail stores struggle to keep their doors open:

1. High Rent Costs:

Retail stores typically require high-rent locations to attract foot traffic, which significantly increases operating costs. Maintaining a physical presence in a prime location can quickly eat into your profits.

2. Declining Foot Traffic:

With the rise of e-commerce, more consumers are shopping online rather than in-person. E-commerce giants like Amazon dominate the market, leading to a steady decline in foot traffic to physical stores.

3. Negative Float:

Retail stores often have to pay for inventory upfront, sometimes seasons in advance. This means you pay for stock long before you see any revenue from it. Additionally, you only make money when customers finally purchase the items, which can take time and disrupt cash flow.

4. Inventory Management:

Predicting which products will sell and managing inventory is challenging. Overstocking or understocking can lead to significant financial losses. Overstocking ties up your capital in unsold goods, while understocking can result in lost sales and unhappy customers.

5. Financial Pitfalls:

- Cash Flow Issues: Retail is often a "cash sucks" business, requiring constant cash input with slow returns.

- Bankruptcies: The retail industry has seen numerous bankruptcies. For example, as of April 2023, eight major retailers, including Bed Bath & Beyond, went bankrupt. This trend highlights the precarious nature of the retail business.

Key Takeaways for Aspiring Retail Store Owners

If you're still determined to open a retail store, here are some strategies to help increase your chances of success:

- **Focus on Niche Markets:** Specialized stores that cater to a specific market or unique products can attract a loyal customer base. Find a niche that isn't overly saturated and offers something unique to your customers.
- **Enhance the Customer Experience:** Create an inviting and memorable shopping experience that can't be replicated online. Offer excellent customer service, engaging store layouts, and in-store events to draw people in.
- **Leverage Technology:** Use technology to streamline operations, manage inventory, and enhance the customer experience. Implementing point-of-sale systems, inventory management

software, and online ordering options can help you stay competitive.
- **Diversify Revenue Streams:** Don't rely solely on in-store sales. Explore additional revenue streams such as online sales, pop-up shops, or collaborations with other local businesses.

Running a retail store in today's digital age is a challenging endeavor. High rent costs, declining foot traffic, and complex inventory management are significant hurdles that require strategic planning and adaptability. However, with a focus on niche markets, exceptional customer experiences, and leveraging technology, it is possible to create a successful retail business.

Chapter 7: Restaurants

The Temptation of Culinary Dreams

Opening a restaurant is a dream shared by many food lovers. The allure of creating a space where people can enjoy delicious meals, share special moments, and experience exceptional service is undeniable. However, the restaurant industry is notoriously tough, with high failure rates and intense competition. The reality of running a restaurant is a challenging mix of high startup costs, cash flow issues, and the constant pressure to keep customers coming back.

Why Restaurants Fail?

Let's break down why so many restaurants struggle to stay open:

1. High Startup Costs:

Building out a restaurant is an expensive endeavor, with costs ranging from $200,000 to $1 million. This high initial investment can drain resources before the restaurant even opens its doors.

2. Cash Flow Issues:

Restaurants often face significant ongoing expenses that can quickly lead to cash flow problems:

- **Wages:** Paying staff is one of the largest expenses for a restaurant. From chefs and servers to dishwashers and managers, labor costs add up quickly.
- **Food Costs:** Constantly buying fresh ingredients is costly, and spoilage is a big problem since food can't be stored indefinitely like non-perishable goods.

3. High Failure Rates:

Statistics show that 60% of restaurants fail within the first year, and 80% within four years. This high failure rate makes the restaurant industry incredibly risky.

4. Intense Competition:

The restaurant market is highly competitive. For example, on a single street, you might find JuiceLand, Chipotle, Hopdoddy, and several other eateries all vying for the same customers. Standing out in such a crowded market is challenging.

5. Customer Retention:

Unlike online businesses where you can gather customer contact information and send them promotions, restaurants typically rely on customers choosing to return on their own. It's challenging to keep customers coming back without direct communication channels.

6. Financial Pitfalls:

 - Lower Resale Value: While the average small business in the US sells for around $800,000, the average restaurant sells for just $198,000. This significant difference reflects the difficulty in maintaining and growing a successful restaurant.

Types of Restaurants and Their Challenges

1. Full-Service Restaurants:

These are more expensive to run and have a higher failure rate. They require a lot of capital for both initial setup and ongoing operations.

2. Fast Food Joints:

These have lower failure rates and are generally more manageable. They require less capital and have more streamlined operations.

Successful Models

Despite the high failure rates, there are successful models in the restaurant industry:

1. Pop-Up Stores:

For example, a restaurant called The Well, which has pop-up stores that are the real profit drivers. These smaller, more flexible units can adapt quickly and generate significant revenue without the high costs associated with full-service restaurants.

2. Food Trucks:

Food trucks have lower startup costs compared to traditional restaurants and offer flexibility in location and menu options. They can be a great way to build a brand and test out concepts before committing to a brick-and-mortar location.

Key Takeaways for Aspiring Restaurant Owners

If you're still passionate about opening a restaurant, here are some tips to help increase your chances of success:

- **Start Small:** Consider starting with a food truck, pop-up, or small takeout restaurant to test your concept and build a customer base before investing in a full-scale restaurant.
- **Focus on Quality and Consistency:** Exceptional food and service are key to retaining customers. Make sure your menu is consistently high quality and that your staff is well-trained.
- **Manage Costs Carefully:** Keep a close eye on expenses, particularly food and labor costs. Efficient inventory management and cost control are crucial.
- **Engage with Your Community:** Build relationships with your local community through events, partnerships, and promotions. Word-of-mouth and local support can be powerful marketing tools.

The restaurant industry is one of the most challenging business ventures, with high startup costs, intense competition, and significant operational hurdles. However, with careful planning, a focus on quality and customer experience, and innovative business models, it is possible to succeed in this vibrant and dynamic industry.

Chapter 8: Trucking and Last Mile Delivery

The Backbone of Modern Commerce

In today's fast-paced, e-commerce-driven world, the demand for reliable and efficient delivery services has never been higher. Trucking and last-mile delivery have become essential components of modern commerce, ensuring that goods reach their final destinations quickly and efficiently. Unlike many other business ventures with high failure rates, trucking and last-mile delivery boast a high success rate, making them a promising opportunity for aspiring entrepreneurs.

Why Last Mile Delivery Succeeds?

Let's explore why the trucking and last-mile delivery industry is thriving:

1. High Demand:

The rise of e-commerce platforms like Amazon has led to a significant increase in the need for last-mile delivery services. Consumers are ordering more online, and they expect their purchases to arrive quickly and reliably. This constant demand creates a steady stream of business for delivery services.

2. High Success Rate:

With a success rate of about 76.4%, last-mile delivery is one of the more reliable sectors to enter. This high success rate is driven by the consistent demand for delivery services and the relatively straightforward business model.

3. Critical Role in Logistics:

Last-mile delivery accounts for 53% of total shipping costs, making it a critical part of the logistics chain. Companies are willing to pay for reliable last-mile delivery to meet consumer expectations and maintain customer satisfaction.

4. Consumer Expectations:

Approximately 90% of consumers expect two to three-day delivery, putting pressure on companies to provide quick and efficient last-mile services. This ongoing pressure ensures a steady demand for delivery businesses.

5. Growing Market Value:

The projected value of the last-mile delivery market is around $84.7 billion, indicating significant growth potential and opportunities for new entrants.

Business Models in Last Mile Delivery

There are several viable business models within the last-mile delivery sector:

1. Owning Delivery Routes:

You can own routes for established companies like UPS or FedEx. This model involves purchasing or leasing delivery routes and operating under a larger brand's umbrella, which can provide stability and brand recognition.

2. Local Store Deliveries:

Partnering with local stores to handle their delivery needs is another viable model. This can involve contracts with multiple stores to provide consistent delivery services, creating a steady revenue stream.

3. In-House Delivery Fleets:

Many companies rely on in-house delivery fleets, but about 42% require additional help from last-mile delivery services. This creates opportunities for third-party providers to fill in the gaps.

Financial Considerations

While the last-mile delivery business is promising, there are financial considerations to keep in mind:

1. Initial Investment:

Trucks and delivery vehicles can be expensive. Leasing might be a more viable option for those just starting. Consider starting with a smaller fleet and scaling up as your business grows.

2. Operational Costs:

Finding and retaining good drivers is crucial. Additionally, vehicle maintenance, fuel costs, and insurance can add up. Efficient route planning and vehicle management can help keep these costs under control.

3. Technology Integration:

Investing in technology to streamline operations, track deliveries, and manage logistics can improve efficiency and customer satisfaction. The future might also bring autonomous delivery vehicles, reducing the need for drivers but requiring significant upfront investment in technology.

Career Opportunities

For those looking to enter the delivery business, there are several career paths and opportunities:

1. Courier Services:
Starting a courier service can be a lower-cost entry point. This model is similar to ride-sharing but often involves certified deliveries, allowing you to charge more.

2. Scalability:
The business can scale with the size of your fleet. Starting with smaller vehicles and gradually moving to larger trucks can help manage growth and investment.

Key Takeaways for Aspiring Delivery Business Owners

If you're considering entering the trucking and last-mile delivery business, here are some tips to increase your chances of success:

- **Invest in Technology:** Use technology to optimize routes, track deliveries, and manage logistics. Efficient operations can help reduce costs and improve customer satisfaction.
- **Focus on Customer Service:** Reliable and timely deliveries are crucial. Building a reputation for excellent service can lead to repeat business and referrals.

- **Start Small and Scale:** Begin with a smaller fleet to manage initial costs and gradually expand as demand increases and your business grows.

The trucking and last-mile delivery industry presents a promising opportunity for aspiring entrepreneurs. High demand, a critical role in logistics, and a growing market make this sector one of the more reliable and profitable business ventures. By investing in technology, focusing on customer service, and scaling strategically, you can build a successful delivery business.

Chapter 10: Real Estate Rental Properties

The Timeless Appeal of Real Estate

Real estate has long been considered a reliable and profitable investment. Owning rental properties is seen as a pathway to financial independence, offering a steady income stream and potential for significant wealth accumulation. Unlike many other business ventures, rental properties boast a high success rate, making them an attractive option for aspiring entrepreneurs and investors alike.

Why Rental Properties Succeed?

Let's explore why rental properties are often a winning investment:

1. High Success Rate:

The success rate for rental properties is about 85.3%, indicating that they rarely go bankrupt compared to other businesses. This high success rate is driven by the consistent demand for housing and the potential for steady rental income.

2. Growing Market:

There are 44 million renters in the US, and this number is increasing. The rental market is substantial and continues to grow, providing a large pool of potential tenants.

3. High Rental Income:

Americans spend $485 billion annually on rent. Often, renting is more expensive on a monthly basis than owning, which benefits landlords. This steady stream of rental income can be a reliable source of cash flow.

4. Incremental Wealth Building:

Landlords can make about $97,000 a year on average. Over time, owning multiple properties can significantly increase income, with "Mom and Pop" landlords owning 20.5 million rental units in the US. Real estate allows for incremental wealth building, as properties appreciate in value over time.

5. Tax Advantages:

Real estate offers various tax advantages, including deductions for mortgage interest, property taxes, and depreciation. These tax benefits can significantly enhance the profitability of rental properties.

Financial Considerations

While rental properties are promising, there are financial considerations to keep in mind:

1. Initial Investment:
Purchasing rental properties requires significant upfront capital, but this can often be financed through mortgages. It's essential to have a solid financial plan and sufficient capital to cover the down payment and initial expenses.

2. Cash Flow Management:
Ensuring you can cover mortgage payments and maintenance costs is crucial. Effective cash flow management is key to avoiding financial troubles. Regularly reviewing and adjusting your budget can help you stay on top of your finances.

3. Maintenance and Repairs:
Owning rental properties comes with the responsibility of maintaining the property and handling repairs. Setting aside a portion of your rental income for maintenance can help you manage these costs without disrupting your cash flow.

Successful Models

There are various models for success in the rental property market:

1. Long-Term Rentals:

Long-term rentals provide a stable, consistent income stream. This model involves renting out properties for extended periods, typically a year or more, to reliable tenants.

2. Short-Term Rentals:

Short-term rentals, such as vacation rentals on platforms like Airbnb, can generate higher income per stay. However, they require more hands-on management and frequent tenant turnover.

3. Multi-Family Units:

Investing in multi-family units, like duplexes or apartment buildings, allows you to maximize rental income from a single property. These properties can provide economies of scale and reduce per-unit maintenance costs.

Key Takeaways for Aspiring Real Estate Investors

If you're considering investing in rental properties, here are some tips to help you succeed:

- **Research the Market:** Understand the local real estate market, including rental demand, property values, and neighborhood dynamics. Knowledge of the market can help you make informed investment decisions.
- **Screen Tenants Carefully:** Finding reliable tenants is crucial. Conduct thorough background checks and reference checks to ensure you rent to responsible individuals who will take care of your property and pay rent on time.
- **Diversify Your Portfolio:** Consider investing in different types of properties and locations to spread your risk. Diversification can help you weather market fluctuations and maintain a steady income stream.
- **Maintain Good Relationships:** Building positive relationships with your tenants can lead to longer tenancies and fewer vacancies. Good communication and prompt attention to maintenance issues can enhance tenant satisfaction.

Investing in rental properties is a proven way to build wealth and achieve financial independence. With a high success rate, growing market, and numerous financial benefits, rental properties offer a reliable and profitable business venture. By researching the market, managing finances effectively, and maintaining good tenant relationships, you can create a successful and sustainable rental property business.

Chapter 11: Laundromats

The Unexpected Goldmine

Laundromats might not seem like the most glamorous business, but they are one of the most resilient and profitable ventures you can invest in. With a remarkably high success rate, laundromats offer steady income, low operational costs, and minimal maintenance, making them an attractive option for aspiring entrepreneurs. Let's dive into why laundromats are such a reliable and lucrative business.

Why Laundromats Succeed?

Let's explore why laundromats often turn out to be successful investments:

1. High Success Rate:

Laundromats have an impressive success rate, typically between 87% and 95%. This high success rate is driven by consistent demand for laundry services and the simplicity of the business model.

2. Low Startup Costs:

Starting a laundromat typically costs between $100,000 and $300,000. This relatively low barrier to entry makes it accessible for many entrepreneurs. Additionally, the durable equipment used in laundromats can last anywhere from 5 to 20 years, providing a long-term investment with minimal maintenance costs.

3. Repeat Customers:

Laundromats attract regular customers who return weekly, ensuring a steady stream of revenue. The need for clean clothes is universal and constant, providing a reliable customer base.

4. Decreasing Competition:

The number of laundromat locations is in decline, reducing competition and potentially increasing the customer base for existing businesses. This trend can create opportunities for those willing to enter the market.

Financial Considerations

While laundromats are promising, there are financial considerations to keep in mind:

1. Initial Investment:

While startup costs are relatively low, it's important to secure enough capital to cover equipment leasing and initial operating expenses. Finding a location with high foot traffic and a large population of renters can significantly impact your success.

2. Operational Costs:

Ongoing costs include utilities, maintenance, and staffing if required. Efficiently managing these expenses can help maximize your profits.

3. Location:

Choosing the right location is crucial for success. High-traffic areas with a large population of renters are ideal. Proximity to apartment buildings and student housing can provide a steady stream of customers.

Additional Revenue Streams

Laundromats are not just resilient businesses with a high success rate; they also offer opportunities for additional revenue streams:

1. Vending Machines:

Installing vending machines on-site can provide a steady stream of extra income. Customers waiting for their laundry are likely to purchase snacks and drinks.

2. ATM Machines:

Having an ATM on-site can also generate additional revenue through transaction fees, especially in areas where cash is commonly used.

3. Wash and Fold Services:

Offering wash and fold services can significantly boost your revenue. This involves staff washing, drying, and folding customers' laundry for a fee, which can range from $30 to $50 per bag. The costs are minimal compared to the high margins.

4. Delivery Services:

Adding delivery services can further enhance revenue. By offering to pick up and drop off laundry, you can tap into a market of busy professionals and families who value convenience.

Technology Integration

Using technology to automate and monitor laundromat operations can reduce the need for staff and increase efficiency:

1. Automation and Monitoring:

Implementing systems that allow customers to pay via mobile apps and monitor machine availability online can improve the customer experience and attract more business. Automated systems can also streamline operations from cash collection to dispensing soap.

2. Customer Convenience:

Providing amenities like free Wi-Fi, comfortable seating, and clean facilities can enhance the customer experience and encourage repeat business.

Key Takeaways for Aspiring Laundromat Owners

If you're considering investing in a laundromat, here are some tips to help you succeed:

- **Choose the Right Location:** High-traffic areas with a large population of renters are ideal for a laundromat. Proximity to residential buildings, colleges, and busy streets can drive consistent business.
- **Invest in Durable Equipment:** High-quality machines that last longer and require less maintenance can save you money in the long run.
- **Offer Additional Services:** Diversifying your revenue streams with vending machines, wash and fold services, and delivery options can significantly boost your income.
- **Leverage Technology:** Implementing modern technology can streamline operations, improve efficiency, and enhance the customer experience.

Laundromats offer a reliable and profitable business opportunity with a high success rate and steady demand. By choosing the right location, investing in durable equipment, and leveraging additional revenue streams, you can create a thriving laundromat business. With careful planning and a focus on customer service, laundromats can be a surprisingly lucrative investment.

A Guide to Choosing the Best Business

1. Self-Assessment: Know Thyself

Before diving into any business venture, it's crucial to conduct a thorough self-assessment. Understanding your own strengths, weaknesses, interests, and risk tolerance will help you choose a business that aligns with your personal and professional goals.

Skills and Interests:

- **Evaluate Your Skills:** What are you good at? Do you have expertise in a particular industry? Your existing skills can be a significant advantage when starting a business.
- **Follow Your Passion:** While passion alone isn't enough to guarantee success, it can be a powerful motivator. Choose a business that you're passionate about, as this will help sustain your motivation through the inevitable ups and downs.

Risk Tolerance:

- **Assess Your Comfort with Risk:** Some businesses are inherently riskier than others. Understand your comfort level with financial and operational risks.

- **Plan Accordingly:** If you're risk-averse, consider businesses with a higher success rate and lower initial investment. If you're willing to take more significant risks for potentially higher rewards, you might explore more volatile industries.

2. Market Research: Understand the Landscape

Thorough market research is essential for identifying viable business opportunities and understanding your potential customer base.

Industry Trends:

- **Stay Informed:** Research current trends in various industries. Look for sectors experiencing growth and those expected to expand in the future.
- **Identify Opportunities:** Find niches or gaps in the market where you can offer something unique or superior.

Target Audience:

- **Know Your Customers:** Identify your target audience and understand their needs, preferences, and behaviors. Tailoring your business to meet these needs can give you a competitive edge.

- **Analyze Competitors:** Study your competitors. Analyze their strengths and weaknesses, and identify opportunities to differentiate your business.

3. Competitive Analysis: Stand Out from the Crowd

Understanding the competitive landscape is crucial for developing a unique value proposition and positioning your business for success.

Competitor Landscape:

- **Study the Competition:** Identify who your competitors are and what they offer. Analyze their business models, marketing strategies, and customer base.
- **Identify Gaps:** Look for gaps in the market that your business can fill. Offering a unique product or service can set you apart from the competition.

Market Gaps:

- **Fill the Void:** Focus on areas where competitors are lacking. Whether it's better customer service, higher quality products, or innovative features, find ways to differentiate your business.

4. Business Model Evaluation: Craft a Winning Strategy

A solid business model is the foundation of a successful venture. Evaluate different business models to find one that aligns with your goals and resources.

Revenue Streams:

- **Diversify Income:** Consider multiple ways to generate revenue. A diversified income stream can provide financial stability and growth opportunities.
- **Maximize Profit:** Focus on high-margin products or services and explore additional revenue streams such as subscriptions, partnerships, or value-added services.

Cost Structure:

- **Analyze Costs:** Understand the costs involved in starting and running the business. Look for models with sustainable profit margins and manageable overheads.
- **Optimize Operations:** Streamline operations to reduce costs and improve efficiency.

5. Legal and Regulatory Considerations: Stay Compliant

Navigating legal and regulatory requirements is essential for avoiding costly fines and ensuring smooth operations.

Licensing and Permits:

- **Get the Right Permits:** Research the licenses and permits required for your chosen business. Ensure you comply with all local, state, and federal regulations.
- **Stay Updated:** Regulations can change, so stay informed about any updates that might affect your business.

Compliance:

- **Understand Regulations:** Familiarize yourself with industry regulations and standards. Non-compliance can lead to legal issues and damage your reputation.
- **Implement Policies:** Develop and implement policies to ensure ongoing compliance with all relevant laws and regulations.

6. Financial Planning: Secure Your Finances

Startup Costs:

Calculate the initial costs of starting the business, including equipment, licenses, and initial inventory. Understanding your startup costs helps you plan your funding and avoid financial pitfalls.

Funding Options:

Explore funding options such as personal savings, loans, grants, or investors. Having a clear financial plan and access to funding is crucial for launching and growing your business.

7. Business Plan Development

Detailed Plan:

Develop a comprehensive business plan outlining your business idea, market analysis, business model, marketing strategy, and financial projections. A well-crafted business plan serves as a roadmap for your business.

SWOT Analysis:

Include a SWOT analysis (Strengths, Weaknesses, Opportunities, Threats) to assess your business's potential. This helps you understand your business's internal and external environment.

8. Location and Infrastructure

Physical vs. Online:

Decide if your business will have a physical location, be online, or a combination of both. The choice depends on your business model and target audience.

Site Selection:

If physical, choose a location that is accessible to your target market and meets your business needs. The right location can significantly impact your success.

9. Technology and Tools

Essential Tools:

Identify the technology and tools you need to run your business efficiently. This could include software for accounting, inventory management, and customer relationship management.

Automation:

Look for opportunities to automate processes to save time and reduce costs. Automation can improve efficiency and allow you to focus on strategic tasks.

10. Marketing Strategy

Branding:

Develop a strong brand identity that resonates with your target audience. A compelling brand can differentiate your business and build customer loyalty.

Promotion:

Plan your marketing and advertising strategies, including digital marketing, social media, and traditional methods. Effective marketing is crucial for attracting and retaining customers.

11. Execution and Adaptation

Launch Plan:

Create a detailed plan for launching your business, including timelines and key milestones. A well-executed launch can set the tone for your business's success.

Feedback and Adaptation:

After launching, continuously gather feedback from customers and be prepared to adapt your strategies based on what you learn. Flexibility and responsiveness are key to long-term success.

Final Thoughts

Choosing the right business involves thorough research, careful planning, and a clear understanding of your strengths and market needs. By following these steps, you can make an informed decision that aligns with your goals and increases your chances of success. Remember, the key to entrepreneurship is flexibility and resilience—be ready to adapt and grow as you navigate your business journey.

Dear Reader,

Thank you for reading " **7 Businesses to Avoid and 4 Winning Opportunities: Your Business Success Guide"** If you're ready to dive deeper into achieving financial freedom, check out my book:

In "**Self-Made Success**" you'll discover:
- Inspiring stories of entrepreneurs who transformed their lives.
- Detailed strategies and actionable steps to build your own successful business.
- Insights from individuals who have successfully navigated the path to financial freedom.

Author Page

Scan The QR Code Above or Visit My **Author Page on Amazon** to Enjoy Your Copy Now.

With gratitude,

Elisabeth Miazello
https://www.amazon.com/author/elisabeth.miazello

Don't Miss Out!

Thank you for reading!
If you found this book helpful, remember to grab your **FREE eBook**:

7 Businesses You Can Start Right Now for Under $1000

Unlock even more opportunities and take your first step towards financial freedom.

Scan the **QR Code** Above or Visit **IRNOX.com/7a** for an Instant Free Download

www.ingramcontent.com/pod-product-compliance
Lightning Source LLC
Chambersburg PA
CBHW030504220526
45464CB00006B/2648